FUN WITH PUZZLES AND PRAYERS

A Catholic Kid's Activity Book

by Geri Berger Haines

Ambassador
Children's Books
New York/Mahwah, NJ

ISBN: 978-0-8091-6751-7

Published by Ambassador Books
An imprint of Paulist Press
997 Macarthur Boulevard
Mahwah, New Jersey 07430

www.ambassadorbooks.com

Printed and bound in the United States of America
by Versa Press, Peoria, IL
January 2010

The Lord's Prayer

Our Father who art in heaven,
hallowed be thy name.
Thy kingdom come.
Thy will be done on earth, as it is in heaven.
Give us this day our daily bread,
and forgive us our trespasses,
as we forgive those who trespass against us,
and lead us not into temptation,
but deliver us from evil. Amen.

The Hail Mary

Hail Mary, full of grace. The Lord is with thee.
Blessed art thou amongst women,
and blessed is the fruit of thy womb, Jesus.
Holy Mary, Mother of God,
pray for us sinners,
now and at the hour of our death. Amen.

The Glory Be

Glory be to the Father,
and to the Son,
and to the Holy Spirit,
as it was in the beginning,
is now, and ever shall be,
world without end. Amen.

Finding Father

Help Tom and Jamie get to their father. All of the streets are one way, so you can only go in the directions of the arrows. First, they have to stop at school. Second, they have to pick up groceries at the market. Third, they have to pick up their dog at the animal clinic, and finally, pick up Dad at work.

Looking Up to Heaven

When we look up at the sky at night, we see the stars and the moon and think of our Father in heaven. The sun shines by day to warm the earth. Find all of the stars, moons, and suns in this picture.

Find the Angels

Angels in heaven are always praising God. God wants us to praise him for his love and mercy. There are eleven angels in this picture. Can you outline and color them? One angel has detached wings, can you find it?

"Our Father" Word Search

The three children are painting pictures of what they think God the Father looks like. What do you think God looks like? Philip, one of Jesus' disciples, asked Jesus to "show us the Father." Jesus said, "Whoever has seen me has seen the Father." Find the words from *The Lord's Prayer* in the puzzle below.

```
L W F Y F U D B O V Z O S X P
E S E S S A P S E R T G A H X
B Y Y L O J P J F X S Z H H B
N Q C I X E R F U F E A R T H
H Q S X N D E W O L L A H D B
E W H X Y F C S T N E V A E H
F X R G A W G M O D G N T K W
O N G N D M I Q W U D I E P V
R M K A A L V T A P A H Q D A
G U R M C C V E W G B F W K F
I Y L E A D R B T E R A L T B
V Z N O I T A T P M E T Z L U
E M U Q U O O L Z S A H K L P
S P V H H M Z G W A D E F I B
E X M O Y M M I T L Y R S W S
```

FATHER
HEAVEN
HALLOWED
NAME
KINGDOM
WILL
EARTH
DAY
BREAD
FORGIVE
TRESPASSES
LEAD
TEMPTATION

7

Find the Face of Jesus

The earth is our home. And it is filled with God's creatures. Find the three angels in the clouds. On the earth, find the girl, boy, dolphin, rabbit, fox, horse, elephant, dove, bear, duck, pig, snake, beaver, bird, fish, cat, snail, and mouse. Can you find the face of Jesus?

Mom's Making Pancakes!

We can all enjoy doing things as a family when we do them out of love. That is what God wants us to do. Find all the things that are different between the two pictures.

Catch the Fish

Some of the apostles made their livelihood as fishermen. Jesus told them they would become fishers of men. God will provide food for us. We are his children. Take the fisherman through the sea to the basket full of fish. Catch as many fish as possible without crossing the waves. Rules: You can cross the outline of a fish (thus catching it), but you cannot cross the waves. It is ok to cross a fish that touches a wave!

Daily Bread

The baker in Jesus' day worked all day long to produce bread for sale, even though many families baked their own bread. How many loaves of bread are in the picture? Find the words below in the puzzle.

BREAD   **OVEN**   **WHEAT**   **FLOUR**   **MEAL**
BAKER   **BARLEY**   **FIRE**   **LOAVES**   **WATER**

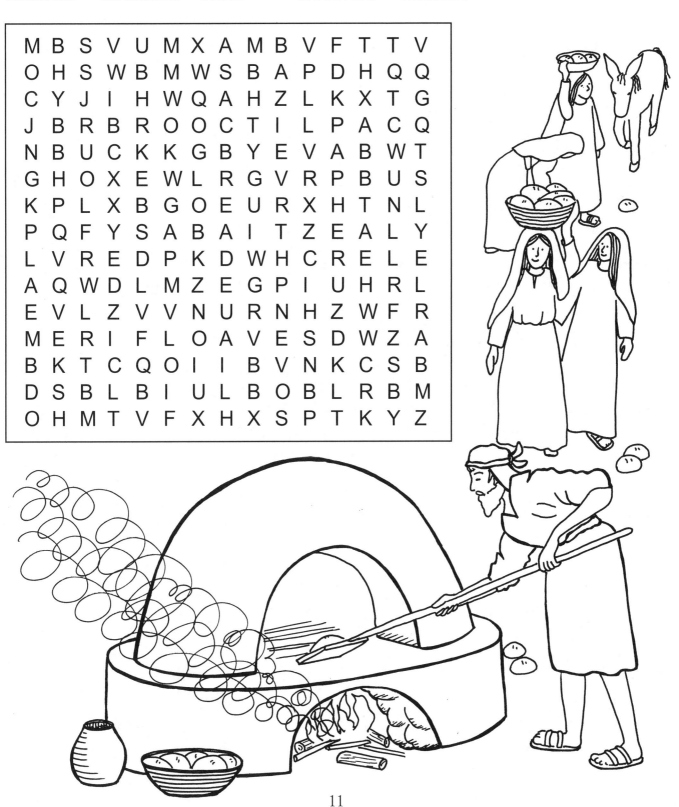

```
M B S V U M X A M B V F T T V
O H S W B M W S B A P D H Q Q
C Y J I H W Q A H Z L K X T G
J B R B R O O C T I L P A C Q
N B U C K K G B Y E V A B W T
G H O X E W L R G V R P B U S
K P L X B G O E U R X H T N L
P Q F Y S A B A I T Z E A L Y
L V R E D P K D W H C R E L E
A Q W D L M Z E G P I U H R L
E V L Z V V N U R N H Z W F R
M E R I F L O A V E S D W Z A
B K T C Q O I I B V N K C S B
D S B L B I U L B O B L R B M
O H M T V F X H X S P T K Y Z
```

Finding Forgiveness

The parable of the Prodigal Son is a story that Jesus told about a boy who left his father. This boy fell into sin, but his father forgave him and ran to welcome him when he saw the boy returning home. Hearts symbolize love. See if you can find all the hearts in the picture.

Finding the Right Path

Temptation is when we feel like doing something we shouldn't do. It can be anything that hurts others or hurts us. And, so we ask God to keep us on the right path because that is what is best for us, makes us happy, and pleases God. Take John and Julie through the maze to get to God the Father.

God the Father

"Hail Mary" Word Search

God blessed Mary to become the mother of Jesus. She is our good friend and someone we can turn to for help. Find the words from the *Hail Mary* in the puzzle.

```
D U Y D Y A X T L R X T B F S
K Y J S R E N N I S W O M B C
F O Q P R A Y F X U T K M P F
E R L O U I V S P S E Y S C S
O N U K Y L O H C E H R X P M
L Q U I Q R R D K J S A H C W
O A Z G T Q N E M I S M X C O
R P F Q Y E X S O P U V S X M
D A F C H Q E S T E C A R G E
H Q U L P P L E H T W S M O N
S D I S I Z M L E G C Q J S G
Y L J L K M L B R N Q K Q H V
V Q I Z H S L F U H M L O A X
K A Z O D M A I I J Z G X H D
H F J C M Y T C Q J Q R R O I
```

HAIL
MARY
GRACE
LORD
BLESSED
WOMEN
FRUIT
WOMB
JESUS
HOLY
MOTHER
PRAY
SINNERS

An Angel Appeared to Mary

"Hail Mary, full of grace. The Lord is with thee." These were the words an angel spoke when it appeared to Mary. The Holy Spirit came upon Mary, and she conceived Jesus. Doves are a symbol of the Holy Spirit. Find the nine doves in the picture.

Slippers for Dad

Being a blessing is showing our love to others in some way. Like Mary, in what way can you be a blessing? Find all the things that are different between the two pictures.

Jesus Is Born

What a joyful time it was when our Savior was born! Angels appeared, and a star was shining in the sky over Bethlehem. Color the picture and give it to someone as a Christmas card.

The Nativity

At Christmastime, the Nativity celebrates the birth of Jesus. We exchange presents, but the Gift that God gave to us was Jesus. Find the following items hidden in the picture: two shepherds with their staffs, the magi (king) with gift, a cat, a mouse, and a pig.

Mary Prays Faithfully

God chose Mary to be the Mother of Jesus because of her humility and holiness. Color the picture of Mary humbly praying.

Mary and Jesus

Circle the two pictures of Mary with baby Jesus that are the same.

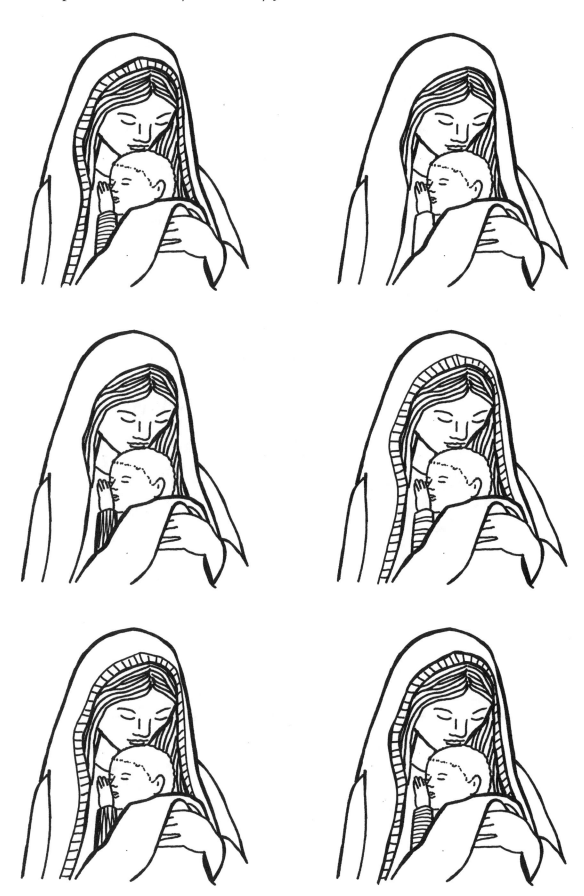

The Glory of God

God's glory shines through the beauty of flowers. Even the insects he created have their own uniqueness and beauty. Find the five insects in the picture. In the puzzle below, find the words from *The Glory Be*.

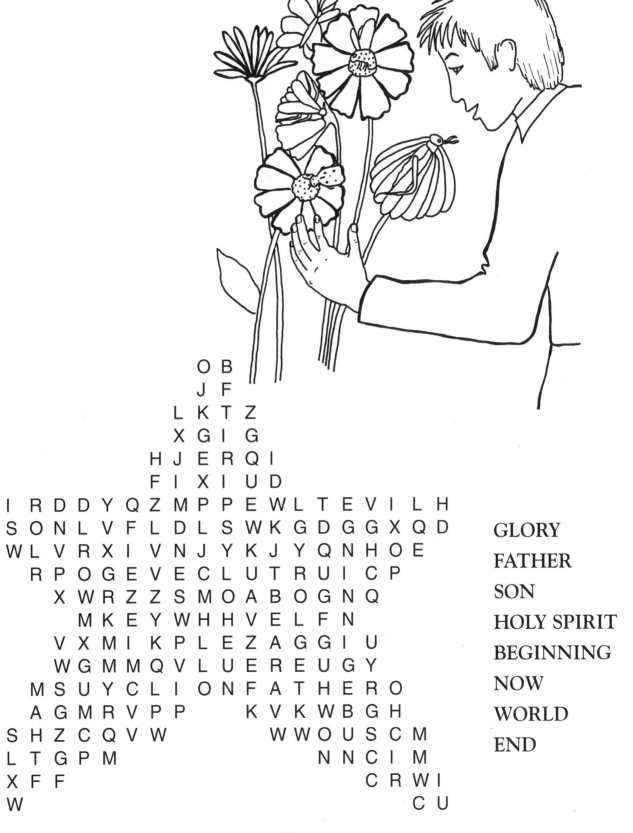

```
                    O B
                    J F
                    L K T Z
                    X G I G
                  H J E R Q I
                  F I X I U D
  S I R D D Y Q Z M P P E W L T E V I L H
  D S O N L V F L D L S W K G D G G X Q D      GLORY
    W L V R X I V N J Y K J Y Q N H O E        FATHER
      R P O G E V E C L U T R U I C P          SON
        X W R Z Z S M O A B O G N Q            HOLY SPIRIT
          M K E Y W H H V E L F N              BEGINNING
        V X M I K P L E Z A G G I U            NOW
      W G M M Q V L U E R E U G Y              WORLD
    M S U Y C L I O N F A T H E R O            END
    A G M R V P P     K V K W B G H
    S H Z C Q V W       W W O U S C M
    L T G P M             N N C I M
  V X F F                   C R W I
  I W                         C U
```

21

Finding God

Finding God is the most important thing we can do in life. Find your way through the maze to the heart.

"J" Is for Jesus

Jesus loves children and children love Jesus. Find the nine words that begin with "J" that are in the picture.

23

Saved from the Flood

God told Noah to build an ark to save two of each animal on the earth from a great flood. In addition to the animals on the ark, how many of these hidden animals can you find? Rabbit, bird, duck, snake, frog, two seals, octopus, two fish, lobster, seahorse, and turtle.

Noah's Ark Crossword Puzzle

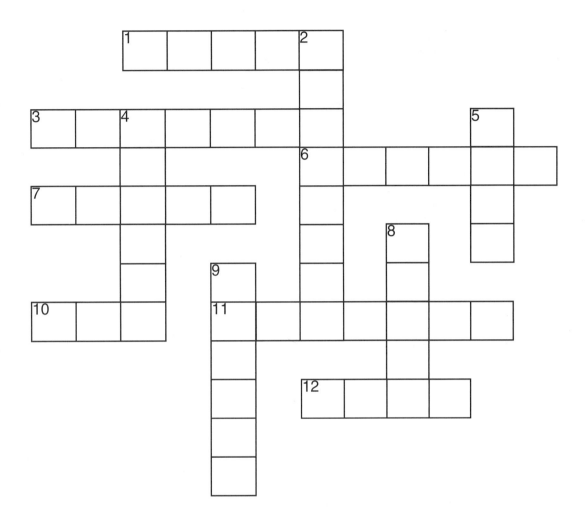

ACROSS

1. Long and slithery creature that moves on its belly.
3. Animal with a very long neck and spots.
6. A bird that repeats words.
7. The striped coat on this animal is a giveaway!
10. A furry house pet.
11. This sea creature will wrap you up with its many tentacles.
12. Kiss this creature and it will turn into a prince!

DOWN

2. One step taken by this animal will squish you flat!
4. Long ears and a cute tail keep this creature hopping.
5. The man who built the ark in the Bible.
8. Short name for a huge land and water creature.
9. A hairy little animal that swings through the trees.

Jesus Loves Children

Match the letter that goes with each child's face to solve the message on the following page.

_____

_____

- - - - - - - - - - - - - - - - - - -

_____

_____

_____

_____

_____

_____

27

Fruitful Vine

The fruits of the Holy Spirit are: love, joy, peace, patience, kindness, goodness, gentleness, faithfulness, self-control. Which numbered branches on the vine lead to each of these fruits?

Say Your Prayers, then Count His Sheep.
God Watches Over You while You Sleep.

Even in all his glory, God cares for every part of your day. Find all the things that are different between the two pictures.

Give Glory to God and Be a Blessing to Others.

Color these cards, and they can be used as Christmas ornaments, or as cards to give to Mom or Dad, or as bookmarks to remind you of God's great love for you.

Answers

Page 4

Page 5

Page 6

Page 7

```
L W F Y F U D B O V Z O S X P
E S E S S A P S E R T G A H X
B Y Y L O J P J F X S Z H H B
N Q C I X E R F U F E A R T H
H Q S X D E W O L L A H D B
E W H X Y F C S T N E V A E H
F X R G A W G M O D G N I K
F O R G N D M I Q W U D I E P V
G U R M K A A L V T A P A H Q D A
R I Y L E A D R B T E R A L T B
I V E Z N O I T A T P M E T Z L
V E M U Q U O O L Z S A H K L I
S P V H H M Z G W A D E F L
E X M O Y M M I T L Y R S W
```

Page 8

Page 9

Page 10

Page 11

```
M B S V U M X A M B V F T T V
O H S W B M W S B A P D H Q Q
C Y J I H W Q A H Z L K X T G
J R B R O O C T I L P A C Q
N B U C K K K G B Y E V A B W T
G H O X E W L R G V R P B U S
K P L X B G O E U R X H T N L
P Q F Y S A B A I T Z E A E Y
L A V R E D P K D W H C R U E L
A Q W D L M Z E G P I U H W R F
E V L Z V V N U R N H Z M F R A
M E R I F L O A V E S D W Z B
B K T C Q O I I B V N K C S
D S B L B I U L B O B L R B M
O H M T V F X H Z S P T K Y Z
```

There are 20 loaves of bread in the picture.

Page 12

Page 13

God the Father

Page 14

```
D U Y D Y A X T L R X T B F S
K Y J S R E N N I S W O M B C
F O Q P R A Y F X U T K M P F
E R L O U I V S P S E Y S C S
O N U K Y L O H S E H R X P M
L Q U I Q R R D K J S A M H C
R D A Z G T Q N E S M I P U S X
A F C H Q E S E O P U V S X
H Q U L P P L E H T W S M O N
S D I S I Z M L E G C Q J G S
Y L J L K M L B R N K Q K H V
V Q I Z H S L F U H M L O A X
K A Z O D M A I I J Z G X H D
H F J C M Y T C Q J Q R R O I
```

Answers

Page 15

Page 21 (top)

Page 21 (bottom)

OBJ
JF
LKGTZ
XGIRG
HJERQI
FIXIUD

S I R D D D Y Q Z M P P E W L T E V I L H
D S O N L V F L D L S Y W K G D G G X Q D
W L V R X I V N J Y K J Y Q N H O E
R P O G E V E C L U T R U G H C P
X W R Z Z S M O A B O G N C N Q
M K E Y W H H V E L U G F G I U
V X M I K P L E Z A G G I Y
W G M M Q V L U E R E U G Y
M S U Y C L I O N F A T H E R O
A G M R V P P K V K W B G H
S H Z C Q V W W W O U S C M
L T G P M N N C I M
V X F F C R W I
I W C U

Page 28

#1 *Self-control*
#2 *Faithfulness*
#3 *Patience*
#4 *Joy and Goodness*
#5 *Kindness*
#6 *Peace*
#7 *Love*
#8 *Gentleness*

Page 16

Page 18

Page 23

Jump rope, jacks, jewelry, jam, juggle,
jungle gym, jog, jug, jingle.

Page 24

Page 27

*Let the little children come to me for of
such is the kingdom of God.*

— Mark 10:14

Page 20

Page 22

Page 25

Page 29